IT LOOKS LIKE A C**K!

IT LOOKS LIKE A C**K!

BEN & JACK

BLOOMSBURY

LONDON · BERLIN · NEW YORK

ABOUT THE AUTHORS

Ben & **J**ack are two ordinary guys, living ordinary lives, with ordinary passions and desires. There is absolutely nothing unusual about the things they like. They enjoy nothing better than to spend their time together searching for the things that they both like, and which are absolutely okay to look for.

A DEDICATION

To our parents, who must be so proud,

AN INTRODUCTION
THIS MUCH WE KNOW

We live in a beautiful, enchanting world,
a startling universe resplendent with a
cornucopia of multitudinous delights —
the laughter of a child; the first rainfall after
an endless, sweltering summer; the twinkling
reflection of a full moon over a calm midnight
lake on a cool autumnal night; a freshly
baked ciabatta, straight from a Tuscan oven,
bristling with peppery salami and just-ripened
avocado, coquettishly handed to you by an
olive-skinned, raven-haired, nubile signorina.

This much we know.

Oh yeah, and there are some things that
look like c**ks.

A DISCLAIMER

BEN AND JACK THINK IT IS IMPORTANT IMAGES CONTAINED WITHIN THIS BOOK NOT FIDDLED WITH IN ANY WAY.

THAT YOU KNOW THAT ALL OF THE
ARE UNMOLESTED, UNTOUCHED AND

THEY ARE AS NATURE INTENDED.

COME FRIENDLY DONGS
AND FALL ON SLOUGH

PROS

Graceful, craning arc and inquisitive
posture suggest questing personality
and good sense of humour.

CONS

It's half a mile away!

48% C**K
PULL OFF AT THE NEXT JUNCTION

LAZY LOB IN THE ARIZONA DESERT

PROS

Impressive rigidity. Inspiring angle
which reminds one of semi-arousal
of supine male.

CONS

Hypertrophic, shaved ballage which
no one likes.

86% CK**
A ROCK AND A HARD PLACE

MARAUDING SKY-DONGER

PROS
Heroic representation. Well-defined
helmet and appropriate shading.

CONS
Heavily distended urethra suggests
botched circumcision as teenager.

94% CK**
IT CAME FROM ABOVE

BAFFLED POLICE SEARCH FOR LEADS AS VIAGRA MUGGERS STRIKE AGAIN

PROS

I never saw it coming. One minute I was walking home through the forest, the next minute I came to with a pounding headache, leaves in my hair, and a dirty great tear in the front of my trousers.

CONS

Stop staring WPC Platt! Can't you see the man's been through enough?

93% C**K

C**KS AND ROBBERS

A C**K IS FOR LIFE,
NOT JUST FOR CHRISTMAS

PROS

We found poor Tito after a call from a
concerned neighbour alerted us to his
dreadful plight. We don't normally take in
cactuses here at the sanctuary, but Tito
was a special case and the other puppies
took to him very quickly.

CONS

A fresh bowl of chow and a good tummy
rub would normally get them out into the
yard, but so far Tito has failed to respond;
although his balls seem to like it.

64% C**K
FOR JUST £2 A MONTH, YOU CAN STOP
US TYING TITO TO A BRICK AND LOBBING
HIM INTO THE CANAL

MAN CAUGHT IN IMPOSSIBLE FELLATIO SCENARIO

PROS
Rare sighting of beautifully proportioned albino thumper. And, for the love of God, he's kissing it!

CONS
Abortive Prince Albert hole and terrifying helmet scars.

53% CK**
HE'S GONNA BLOW!

CHIPPING NORTON'S VILLAGE FETE RUINED BY LATE ENTRY

PROS

Punishing girth, walloping great ballbags, preposterous length, vestigial foreskin doubling as handle… Wow! Oh, and at just under 3ft, this delightful specimen can still be loaded as hand-luggage.

CONS

Precious few to mention. One of those rare, happy instances where criticism would be churlish, like chastising the gardener for growing inappropriate vegetables.

82% C**K
FOR GOD'S SAKE MARJORIE, GET YOUR COAT WE'RE LEAVING

YOU SAY TOMATO, I SAY C**K

PROS

Enthusiastic pubic growth. Lovely,
polished, glossy willy. Edible penis
always a bonus.

CONS

Complete absence of man cherries
and faint air of femininity may point
to this not being a c**k at all.
Overgrown clitoris; run for the hills!

60% CK**
LET'S CALL THE WHOLE THING A BIG UGLY
C**K TOMATO WITH A SCREWY STALK

REARGUARD ACTION BREAKTHROUGH FOR CRACK GERMAN SAUSAGE DIVISION

PROS

For a conventionally solitary, unruly beast, such strength in numbers is a rare and exciting find. Their leader has disciplined his boys well.

CONS

It's as we always feared – the Hun cloned the c**k!

61% C**K
YAR, YAR, PIETER, DAS EINE GROSSEN SAUSAGEHAUSER!

STUNNED PALAEONTOLOGISTS UNEARTH CATEGORICAL EVIDENCE OF THE FABLED C**KOSAURUS

PROS

100% anatomically correct, with inch-perfect ratio of girth to length, accompanied by a lovely big set of knackers that really frame this enchanting scene. And to cap it all, it's a beautiful day for a bike ride.

CONS

The team broke a lot of spades in the rush to reveal this prehistoric marvel. And the poor saps are still digging for the helmet.

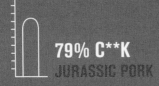

79% CK**
JURASSIC PORK

WELCOME TO
LONDON'S C**KLANDS

PROS

Perfect c**kage with self-cleansing Jap's
Eye courtesy of Old Father Thames.

CONS

A little on the short side. On the
soft? Dresses to the left – hopelessly
out of fashion!

49% CK**

DODGY CKNEY**

ICE GUYS FINISH LAST

PROS
DEAN SEEKS TORVILL : Soft, free-thinking, artistic, with GSOH. Loves animals, long walks, ice-skating. WLTM female with cold hands. What's wrong with just being a really nice guy?

CONS
Hi, it's me. I know we had a great time last night at the rink, but I've realised that I see you more as a friend than anything else. And seriously, this has absolutely nothing to do with your total lack of chestnuts.

31% C**K
IT'S OKAY, WE CAN JUST HOLD HANDS

WHAT DO YOU CALL A MAN WITH A 200FT STONE PENIS?

PROS

No pant could ever claim to tame this monstrous Frankenc**k (although to be fair, none have tried). Erosion has done for the minor body parts, but 'Big Tufty' just won't go down.

CONS

Semi-derelict state has left Big Tufty all alone, save for his patchy and unsettling pubic growth. 'Why you laugh at Big Tufty? Big Tufty have feelings too.'

57% CK**
PAY ATTENTION, HE'S CALLED BIG TUFTY

ROBOC**K

PROS

Too quick with the zipper? Shut yourself in
the shower door? Hang-glided into a cactus?
Your prayers are answered! New Roboc**k
3000 comes equipped with solid steel
thunder stick, 3-speed auto-thruster and
revolutionary jet-powered Detachoballs™ †.

CONS

†Roboc**k Ltd accepts absolutely no
responsibility for spontaneous take-off
of Detachoballs™.

22% CK**
READ INSTRUCTIONS
CAREFULLY BEFORE USE

IF YOU GO DOWN TO THE WOODS TODAY…

PROS

Cleft helmet a real life-saver for those hot, sticky summers, topped off with some excellent filigree work that exhibits a cheeky sense of the absurd.

CONS

Just like Mama's chilli con carne, smooth as silk on the way in, rough as old boots on the way out.

81% CK**
CAN'T SEE THE TREES FOR THE WOOD

ROYAL GARDENER SUSPENDED OVER INSENSITIVE PLANTING FOR BALMORAL GARDEN PARTY

PROS

Placed in convivial surroundings and given time to mature, this cross-gartered, multi-balled exotic makes for a lovely conversation piece. Shame, Princess Di would have loved it...

CONS

The party was bumping along swimmingly until that scamp Prince Edward gave it a little tickle and all hell broke loose. The corgis shat up the Land Rover, Philip chinned Andrew, and Her Majesty's holed herself up in the rumpus room.

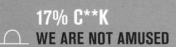

17% C**K
WE ARE NOT AMUSED

FROZEN JEWISH CLACKER RIDES THE SEVEN SEAS

PROS
Crisp, deep and even sculpture of classic communal shower c**k (turn 90 degrees). Gives global warming a good name.

CONS
Unnerving combination of young man's 'head' on old man's 'shoulders'.

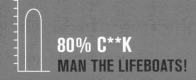

80% CK**
MAN THE LIFEBOATS!

DR PENISTONE, I PRESUME

PROS

Day 27: Dearest Jenkins, I write to you in a state of extreme arousal. We came across the mighty Wang-Tu-Tu this morning, mercifully sleeping off the exertions of the night before. The wager is won, the museum is saved and you might want to put down fresh sawdust in the guest bedroom.

CONS

Such was the ferocity of the encounter that my hitherto trusted companion Matubu turned heel and legged it into the scrub, taking with him my good trousers, an ounce of raspberry shag and what was left of the Kendal mint cake.

76% C**K
CAGING THE BEAST

JOHNSON 3:16

PROS

For God so loved the world that He thrust upon us His terrifying tumescence so we might feel humbled and insecure every time we drop our undercrackers.

CONS

And lo, on the fourth day God regretted His childish prank, and there was very little rejoicing.

8% C**K
ALL HAIL THE SECOND COMING

FEMALE GOLF PROFESSIONAL CELEBRATES LATEST VICTORY AND TAKES HOME YETI'S MEAT

Delicate, reverential handling exhibits rightful respect for this frankly awesome locker room favourite.

Rectangular scrotum, dimpled bell-end, overly planed shaft – home DIY enthusiast?

83% C**K

JUST WHEN YOU THOUGHT IT WAS SAFE TO GO BACK IN THE WATER

PROS

'Understand this Chief. I'm the Mayor of this town and you must be one clam short of a Vongole if you think I'm going to close down the beaches because you've seen another man-eater in the water.'

CONS

'Don't you see? This ain't no kissy-girl dolphin, this ain't no faggoty shark, this is a c**k, goddammit! Have you seen what these things can do to people? Now, I'm gonna need a fishing rod, a pair of thigh-high waders, and a laminated picture of your wife.'

45% C**K
THAT WAS NO BOAT ACCIDENT

RUGBY TEAM ILL AT EASE WITH REFEREE'S UNORTHODOX APPROACH TO PRE-MATCH STUD INSPECTION

PROS

Match-winning thunder thighs leading up to a streamlined set of buns so tight you could bounce a pound coin off them.

CONS

Hairy ass crack a definite hazard in the scrum. Sin bin: 10 minutes.

73% C**K
CROUCH. TOUCH. PAUSE. ENGAGE.

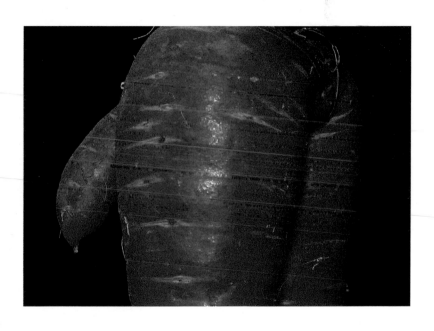

GOODNESS, GRACIOUS, GREAT BALLS OF FIRE

PROS

Crimson red, unspoiled, virginal package, just ripe for the picking. Dimpled surface area will control overheating and prevent the torture of Betty Swollocks (and associated chafing).

CONS

The splendour of this guy's mighty stones suggest that he's been waiting patiently for Ms Right. CODE RED! The next girl to turn on this tiny tap better have her skirt tucked into her knickers.

61% C**K
POPPING THE CHERRY

OUT AND ABOUT WITH GORDON GEKKO'S WANG

PROS

A handsome, gregarious go-getter.
Top of the range executive penis to
subdue ambitious underlings and
boardroom flare-ups.

CONS

Completely inconsiderate and highly
impractical. For business use only.

73% C**K
REAL MEN DON'T EAT QUICHE

WIDOW DISTRAUGHT AS HUSBAND'S WAKE IS EMPTIED BY SON-IN-LAW'S TASTELESS OFFERING

PROS

Hi. Can I order a floral tribute, mainly blue and white flowers? I don't know, say seventy roses with a bit of foliage. Oh, and, can you make it in the shape of a c**k, please.

CONS

Not good enough for your daughter, was I? Hope you like the flowers you old dead bastard.

65% CK**
IS NOTHING SACRED?

GEORGE HARRISON'S LOVE WAND HEADLINES BEATLES MEMORABILIA AUCTION

PROS

A unique chance to own this very special portion of the Fab Four. Practically in mint condition, George's infamous chopper was reputedly inspiration for such memorable hits as 'Come Together', 'Don't Let Me Down', 'The Long and Winding Road', 'You've Got to Hide Your Love' and 'Norwegian Wood'.

CONS

Sadly, the certificate of authenticity was misplaced in transit, but Ringo says that this is definitely George's rhythm stick.

37% C**K
ALL YOU NEED IS LOVE

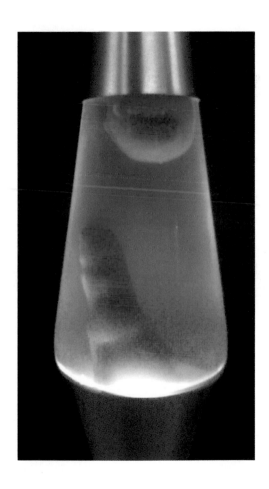

PORKY'S APPRECIATION SOCIETY BANNED BY HARVARD AFTER DEAN'S OFFICE 'DONGED'

PROS

Look guys, I'm a big fan of the movie too, and don't think I can't appreciate the ingenuity that went into turning my best Egyptian cotton sheets into that handsome window wanger. And, by the way, the venting in the helmet? Inspired.

CONS

But after you guys concealed yourselves in the cavity wall of the ladies' shower block AND rigged up my wife's dressing room with a live webcam, I'm afraid you've taken the decision out of my hands. You brought it on yourselves boys – the PAS has shot its last bolt.

34% C**K
MAGNA CUM LAUDE

FIELD OF DREAMS

PROS
Gargantuan proportions make this
the perfect pilgrimage site for all
lovers of the blue-veined flute.

CONS
Being only visible from the air makes
this Jolly Green Giant the preserve
of the privileged few.

69% C**K
IF YOU MOW IT, IT WILL COME

STREET SWEEPERS WALK OUT AFTER SEWAGE WORKERS' PRACTICAL JOKE TAKES A NASTY TURN

PROS

'Come on lads, where's your sense of humour? It's only a little one. You're lucky we didn't send the balls up.'

CONS

'It's a hard enough job at the best of times without steel penises coming at you at 100 miles an hour. That last one those idiots fired up split my broom and nearly knocked my dustcart over.'

71% CK**
ONE MAN'S MEAT IS
ANOTHER MAN'S POISON

THE BIGGER THEY COME, THE HARDER THEY FALL

PROS

Come on big fella, don't let them see you like this. Of course they're gonna say nasty things, they're jealous. Remember what they always say, 'It's nice to put on Speedos when you're hung like a torpedo.'

CONS

Jesus, if this is what you're like when you're sad, I'd hate to see you when you're happy. And don't think you're getting a hug either.

64% CK**

DON'T BEAT YOURSELF OFF OVER IT

NEW BRANCH OF CONTROVERSIAL CHURCH OF C**KOLOGY OFF TO SLOW START

PROS

Founded upon the teachings of Bhagwan Shree Tom Selleck, C**kology preaches the compulsory wearing of short towelling dressing-gowns, the euphoria of high-waisted tight jeans and some other weird stuff about aliens and chest wigs and arousing topiary.

CONS

We've been open for 3 weeks and all we've got is Shaggy and Scooby sitting out there stoned in the hippie wagon. Better call Selleck's brother and tell him the talk's off.

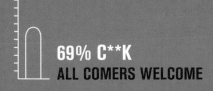

69% CK**
ALL COMERS WELCOME

YOUNG BRIDE SUMMONS EXORCIST AS X-RATED HAUNTING CONTINUES

PROS

Father, it happened again last night, exactly like before. Soon after my husband came to bed, I heard the toilet flush, there was a rustling under the covers, followed by a loud groan, then a big, hot wad of something hit me in the face.

CONS

Hush my child, everything will be fine. Sexorcisms like this are simple affairs: pop a bottle of wine in the chiller, put on some Enya, run a hot, soapy bath, and I'll slip on a cassock and my best crucifix and be round in half an hour.

20% C**K
IT CAME FROM BEYOND

IS IT A BIRD, IS IT A PLANE…?

PROS

By day a mild-mannered, cheese-shaped office block, by night a 400ft crime-fighting brick dick.

CONS

Massive concrete foundations and underground car park mean that unless the crime occurs within the immediate vicinity, this frustrated daredevil is of absolutely no use.

48% C**K
NO, IT'S CAPTAIN STIFFY!

ANIMAL, VEGETABLE, MINERAL...
PENIS?

PROS

Stuffed with lean mince and topped with a melted
Dutch gouda, this hot and handsome devil makes
for an electric accompaniment to a pigeon breast
and cous cous main. Bon appetit!

CONS

Woah there big fella, this dirty beast is for dinner with
your mistress, not supper with the wife. Remember,
it's your children she's kissing with that mouth.

62% C**K
TASTE THE DIFFERENCE

UNUSUAL NEW VENDING MACHINE A SURPRISE SENSATION IN DOWNTOWN DALLAS

PROS

The Derringer – Great for sports and tight, tight shorts: $50

Colt 45 – Versatile yet with imposing heft. Although mostly a social penis, this sharp-shooter won't let you down between the sheets: $100

44 Magnum – It'll blow your head clean off!: $200

CONS

Customers are advised not to drink, drive or operate heavy machinery while wielding the 44 Magnum.

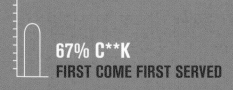

67% C**K
FIRST COME FIRST SERVED

MAVERICK CEO STANDS ALONE IN DEBATE ON THE MOTIVATIONAL POWERS OF HAVING A GREAT BIG C**K IN THE LOBBY

PROS

Machine-cut scrotum ensures perfectly rounded, revolving ballage and provides an ideal launchpad for ergonomically designed shaft, which will heighten productivity whilst reducing operator fatigue and discomfort, which is lovely.

CONS

Stair access to 'Biffin's Bridge' is useful for inspection and storage etc. But in practice the whole endeavour is a flaming assault on decency and smacks of corporate arrogance on a grand scale. Blue sky thinking my arse.

42% C**K
REMEMBER GUYS, PEOPLE LAUGHED AT CHRIS COLUMBUS WHEN HE SAID 'I'M OFF TO AMERICA'. WHO'S LAUGHING NOW?

MIRROR, MIRROR ON THE WALL, WHO'S GOT THE BIGGEST WANGER OF ALL?

PROS

The other dwarfs never believed Snow White when she said there was something special about Dopey, until that morning in the showers.

CONS

Bad news – size does matter.

58% C**K
WHISTLE WHILE YOU JERK

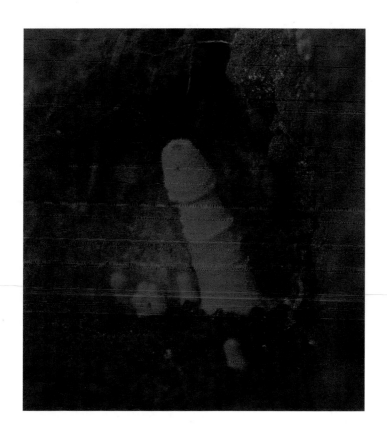

I WANDERED SEXY AS A CLOUD

PROS

Ladies, I can tell you lookin' and I know you like what you see. And I know what you askin' yourselves and the answer is yes – I'm all natural. Now charter a goddamn 747 and get your asses up here.

CONS

It gets so lonely up here, the only ladies I meet are air hostesses, and don't think I can't hear them screamin' through them Pyrex windows.

78% C**K
BABY, IT'S MY DUTY, AND I'M ALWAYS FREE

CALIFORNIA-BASED IMPOTENCY CLINIC UNVEILS CONTROVERSIAL NEW 'C**K GARDEN'

PROS

Here at the Ironman Clinic, we're all about personal growth. Our guests kick off the morning with a stimulating breakfast of 20 oysters and 3 pints of Guinness. Then it's straight into our private cinema for a 3 hour European pornfest. After a light snack lunch, the highlight of the day comes with a stirring 5 hour rock-hugging session in the garden.

CONS

Matron was positive she saw an erection last week, but unfortunately she also had to deal with 5 cases of extreme heat exhaustion and 27 cases of food poisoning. As of next week we'll be changing our caterers.

54% CK**
REACH FOR THE SKIES

EARLY PROTOTYPE FOR ABANDONED WAR C**K

PROS

Phenomenal bell-end, gratifyingly
disproportionate to lean shaft and
surrounding vegetation. Cunningly
placed release valve to alleviate
symptoms of blue balls.

CONS

A showpiece c**k, which requires
military clearance and small crane
for use.

76% CK**

MAKE LOVE NOT WAR

F**K NOSE WHAT'S GOING ON HERE

PROS
What you see is what you get.
This lucky dude wears his heart on
his sleeve and his c**k on his face.
Ladies, form an orderly queue.

CONS
Undescended left bollock could lead to
complications in later life. Caution! When
erect, subject's vision is totally obscured.

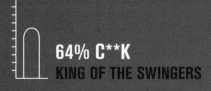

64% CK**
KING OF THE SWINGERS

WHO PUT THIS ONE IN HERE?

PROS

It looks quite bendy. Is that good?

CONS

Ah man, there's just so much wrong with it. It's got little legs, some weird rocky thing where its pubes should be and it moves so slowly it's gonna be around for ages. And why is it so wet…?

0% C**K
WELL, THAT JUST ABOUT
RUINS THE WHOLE BOOK

PICTURE ACKNOWLEDGMENTS

Ben & **J**ack would like to thank the following for providing photographs. While every effort has been made to trace and acknowledge all copyright holders, we would like to apologise should there have been any errors or omissions, unless you're that asshole who didn't get back to us after we emailed you 15 times.

Ice Guys Finish Last – Jonathan Bein
Lazy Lob – dpd photo
(www.flickr.com/photos/dpdphoto)
200ft Penis – Juho Vähä-Herttua
Marauding Sky Donger – Jodie Hunter
Field of Dreams – Duncan Brooks
You Say Tomato – Paul Fontana
A C**k is For Life – Jay Freeman
German Sausage Division – Christiane Moore
(www.christiane.paperpetual.com)
Mirror, Mirror On the Wall – Traci Clevenger
Balls of Fire – Mireille Sillander
Johnson 3:16 – Henry M K Diaz
Just When You Thought It Was Safe – Matthieu Collomp
Who Put This One in Here? – Amanda Sipa

Roboc**k – Keith Meng-wei Loh
Sexy As a Cloud – James Dobson
George Harrison's Love Wand – Jim
The Harder They Come – Josh Homme
Street Sweepers – Gabi Helfert
Royal Gardener Suspended – Christina Pedersen
Animal, Vegetable, Mineral – James Broad
(www.flickr.com/photos/kulor)
Church of C**kology – Stacy Cochrell
Slough – Jack (Ben driving)
Chipping Norton Village Fete – Graham Samuel
Frozen Jewish Clacker – Rex Features
Impossible Fellatio Scenario – Corbis
C**klands – Courtesy of the TopSat consortium
© QinetiQ
F**k Nose – Corbis
Female Golf Pro – Empics
Rugby Team Ill At Ease – Rex Features
Dr Penistone – Jason J. Corneveaux
Is It a Bird – Marina Silva
Distraught Widow – Laura Riseam
Maverick CEO – Ben
(Jack holding legs and Shane Allen spotting)

ACKNOWLEDGMENTS

Ben & **J**ack would like to thank:
Antony Topping; Daniel Greenberg; Richard Atkinson and all
at Bloomsbury; Marc Resnick and all at St Martins Press;
the design genius of Unreal; Richard Bravery; Michelle Kane;
Jamie H-W; Jess, Ellie and Theo; Chairman, Chairwoman, Ben
and Anna; and, of course, Simon Collins for his monkey magic.

First published in Great Britain 2009

Copyright © 2009 by Ben Dunn and Jack Fogg

The moral right of the authors has been asserted!

Bloomsbury Publishing Plc, 36 Soho Square, London W1D 3QY

Bloomsbury Publishing, London, New York and Berlin

A CIP catalogue record for this book is available from the British Library

ISBN 978 1 4088 0245 8

10 9 8 7 6 5 4 3 2 1

Designed by the Members of Unreal, 20 Rugby Street, London, WC1N 3QZ
www.unrealdesign.co.uk

Printed in China

All papers used by Bloomsbury Publishing are natural, recyclable products
made from wood grown in well-managed forests. The manufacturing processes
conform to the environmental regulations of the country of origin.

www.bloomsbury.com